THIS BOOK BELONGS TO:

_____

_____

PLUSHTECH™ and Rohi AI™ are pending trademarks of Plush Education,
What a fun way to live © Plush Education, 2025 All rights reserved.
Rohikids.com

Welcome to Reading & Writing Adventures! This book is your exciting guide to exploring the wonderful world of words. Inside, you'll find fun activities that will help you become a reading and writing expert. We'll focus on sight words, which are special words you see often when you read.

Sight words are important because they help you read more quickly and easily. Instead of sounding them out, you can recognise them right away! In this book, you'll learn 100 sight words that will make reading smoother and more fun.

Each page is filled with fun ways to help you learn and remember sight words. You'll get better every day, and soon you'll know these words like a pro!

Are you ready for your adventure?

Let's Begin!

© Plush Education

BENEFITS OF THIS BOOK:

- Improves reading fluency – Kids can read faster without stopping to sound out each word.

- Builds reading confidence – Recognising words easily makes reading feel easier and more fun.

- Supports comprehension – When children don't have to focus on decoding, they can understand the story better.

- Helps with writing – Knowing sight words makes it easier to spell and write sentences.

- Expands vocabulary – Sight words are common in books, so learning them increases word knowledge.

- Encourages independent reading – Kids feel proud and motivated when they can read on their own.

- Lays a strong foundation – Mastering sight words prepares children for more complex reading skills.

© Plush Education

SIGHT WORDS

Every big writer starts with little letters - keep going, you're doing great!

1 READ IT!

a

Say the word out loud.

2 COLOR IT!

a

Color in the word.

3 TRACE IT!

a

Trace the word.

4 WRITE IT!

Write the word.

5 SPELL IT!

Spell the word.

6 CLAP IT!

1   2   3

How many syllables are in the word? Color in the correct number.

7 FIND IT!

Find the word and color it in.

an	a	at
a	all	a

8 TELL IT!

Who did you tell?

Go tell someone the word!

© Plush Education

1

SIGHT WORDS

Mistakes help you grow - write, learn, and shine brighter each day!

1 READ IT!
am

Say the word out loud.

2 COLOR IT!
am

Color in the word.

3 TRACE IT!
am

Trace the word.

4 WRITE IT!

Write the word.

5 SPELL IT!

Spell the word.

6 CLAP IT!
1 2 3

How many syllables are in the word?
Color in the correct number.

7 FIND IT!
Find the word and color it in.

an	am	off
am	all	am

8 TELL IT!
Who did you tell?

_____

Go tell someone the word!

© Plush Education

SIGHT WORDS

"Your words are powerful - every letter you write tells your special story!"

1 READ IT!

an

Say the word out loud.

2 COLOR IT!

an

Color in the word.

3 TRACE IT!

an

Trace the word.

4 WRITE IT!

Write the word.

5 SPELL IT!

☐ ☐

Spell the word.

6 CLAP IT!

① ② ③

How many syllables are in the word? Color in the correct number.

7 FIND IT!

Find the word and color it in.

an	am	an
at	an	at

8 TELL IT!

Who did you tell?

_____

Go tell someone the word!

© Plush Education

SIGHT WORDS

Writing is an adventure - grab your pencil and let your imagination fly!

1 READ IT!

as

Say the word out loud.

2 COLOR IT!

as

Color In the word.

3 TRACE IT!

as

Trace the word.

4 WRITE IT!

Write the word.

5 SPELL IT!

Spell the word.

6 CLAP IT!

1   2   3

How many syllables are In the word?
Color In the correct number.

7 FIND IT!

Find the word and color it in.

at	as	am
as	an	as

8 TELL IT!

Who did you tell?

_____

Go tell someone the word!

© Plush Education

SIGHT WORDS

"Keep writing - every word you write is a step forward!"

1 READ IT!

at

Say the word out loud.

2 COLOR IT!

at

Color in the word.

3 TRACE IT!

at

Trace the word.

4 WRITE IT!

Write the word.

5 SPELL IT!

Spell the word.

6 CLAP IT!

1 2 3

How many syllables are in the word?
Color in the correct number.

7 FIND IT!

Find the word and color it in.

at	at	as
am	at	an

8 TELL IT!

Who did you tell?

_____

Go tell someone the word!

© Plush Education

SIGHT WORDS

Sight words are your reading superpower — use them wisely!

1 READ IT!

be

Say the word out loud.

2 COLOR IT!

be

Color In the word.

3 TRACE IT!

be

Trace the word.

4 WRITE IT!

_____

Write the word.

5 SPELL IT!

☐ ☐

Spell the word.

6 CLAP IT!

① ② ③

How many syllables are In the word? Color In the correct number.

7 FIND IT!

Find the word and color it in.

| be | be | bee |
| so | be | no |

8 TELL IT!

Who did you tell?

_____

Go tell someone the word!

© Plush Education

6

SIGHT WORDS

Practice makes progress — you're getting better every day!

1 READ IT!

by

Say the word out loud.

2 COLOR IT!

by

Color in the word.

3 TRACE IT!

by

Trace the word.

4 WRITE IT!

Write the word.

5 SPELL IT!

☐ ☐

Spell the word.

6 CLAP IT!

① ② ③

How many syllables are in the word? Color in the correct number.

7 FIND IT!

Find the word and color it in.

by	y	by
bit	by	bee

8 TELL IT!

Who did you tell?

_____

Go tell someone the word!

7

© Plush Education

SIGHT WORDS

"Don't give up — great writers start with small letters!"

1. READ IT!
can
Say the word out loud.

2. COLOR IT!
can
Color in the word.

3. TRACE IT!
can
Trace the word.

4. WRITE IT!

Write the word.

5. SPELL IT!
☐ ☐ ☐
Spell the word.

6. CLAP IT!
① ② ③
How many syllables are in the word? Color in the correct number.

7. FIND IT!
Find the word and color it in.

| can | call | can |
| cool | cap | can |

8. TELL IT!
Who did you tell?

_____

Go tell someone the word!

© Plush Education

8

SIGHT WORDS

Every time you write, you grow stronger and smarter.

1 READ IT!

do

Say the word out loud.

2 COLOR IT!

do

Color in the word.

3 TRACE IT!

do

Trace the word.

4 WRITE IT!

Write the word.

5 SPELL IT!

Spell the word.

6 CLAP IT!

1 2 3

How many syllables are in the word?
Color in the correct number.

7 FIND IT!

Find the word and color it in.

| do | do | die |
| dorm | dor | do |

8 TELL IT!

Who did you tell?

_____

Go tell someone the word!

© Plush Education

SIGHT WORDS

Reading sight words helps you read faster and better!

1. READ IT!

go

Say the word out loud.

2. COLOR IT!

go

Color in the word.

3. TRACE IT!

go

Trace the word.

4. WRITE IT!

Write the word.

5. SPELL IT!

Spell the word.

6. CLAP IT!

1   2   3

How many syllables are in the word? Color in the correct number.

7. FIND IT!

Find the word and color it in.

go	goal	gone
got	go	go

8. TELL IT!

Who did you tell?

_____

Go tell someone the word!

© Plush Education

10

SIGHT WORDS

You can do it — just one word at a time!

1. READ IT!
he
Say the word out loud.

2. COLOR IT!
he
Color in the word.

3. TRACE IT!
he
Trace the word.

4. WRITE IT!
Write the word.

5. SPELL IT!
Spell the word.

6. CLAP IT!
1 2 3
How many syllables are in the word? Color in the correct number.

7. FIND IT!
Find the word and color it in.

| hi | he | he |
| he | hand | him |

8. TELL IT!
Who did you tell?

Go tell someone the word!

© Plush Education

11

SIGHT WORDS

"Believe in your words — they matter!"

1 READ IT!

I

Say the word out loud.

2 COLOR IT!

I

Color In the word.

3 TRACE IT!

I

Trace the word.

4 WRITE IT!

Write the word.

5 SPELL IT!

Spell the word.

6 CLAP IT!

1 2 3

How many syllables are In the word?
Color In the correct number.

7 FIND IT!

Find the word and color it in.

is	It	I
I	id	It

8 TELL IT!

Who did you tell?

Go tell someone the word!

© Plush Education

SIGHT WORDS

"Mistakes are proof you're trying — keep going!"

1 READ IT!

if

Say the word out loud.

2 COLOR IT!

if

Color in the word.

3 TRACE IT!

if

Trace the word.

4 WRITE IT!

Write the word.

5 SPELL IT!

☐ ☐

Spell the word.

6 CLAP IT!

① ② ③

How many syllables are in the word?
Color in the correct number.

7 FIND IT!

Find the word and color it in.

if	it	if
in	if	in

8 TELL IT!

Who did you tell?

_____

Go tell someone the word!

© Plush Education

SIGHT WORDS

Writing is fun — let your pencil dance!

1 READ IT!

in

Say the word out loud.

2 COLOR IT!

in

Color in the word.

3 TRACE IT!

in

Trace the word.

4 WRITE IT!

Write the word.

5 SPELL IT!

Spell the word.

6 CLAP IT!

1   2   3

How many syllables are in the word?
Color in the correct number.

7 FIND IT!

Find the word and color it in.

| in | it | if |
| in | is | in |

8 TELL IT!

Who did you tell?

Go tell someone the word!

© Plush Education

SIGHT WORDS

You're a word explorer — find and use new words!

1 READ IT!

is

Say the word out loud.

2 COLOR IT!

is

Color in the word.

3 TRACE IT!

is

Trace the word.

4 WRITE IT!

Write the word.

5 SPELL IT!

Spell the word.

6 CLAP IT!

How many syllables are in the word? Color in the correct number.

7 FIND IT!

Find the word and color it in.

is	in	if
is	is	it

8 TELL IT!

Who did you tell?

_____

Go tell someone the word!

© Plush Education

SIGHT WORDS

"Sight words make reading easy — you've got this!"

1 READ IT!

it

Say the word out loud.

2 COLOR IT!

it

Color in the word.

3 TRACE IT!

it

Trace the word.

4 WRITE IT!
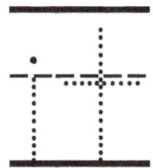

Write the word.

5 SPELL IT!

Spell the word.

6 CLAP IT!

1 2 3

How many syllables are in the word?
Color in the correct number.

7 FIND IT!

Find the word and color it in.

it	it	if
in	in	it

8 TELL IT!

Who did you tell?

_____

Go tell someone the word!

© Plush Education

16

SIGHT WORDS

Write bravely, read proudly!

1 READ IT!
may

Say the word out loud.

2 COLOR IT!
may

Color in the word.

3 TRACE IT!
may

Trace the word.

4 WRITE IT!

Write the word.

5 SPELL IT!

☐ ☐ ☐

Spell the word.

6 CLAP IT!
① ② ③

How many syllables are in the word?
Color in the correct number.

7 FIND IT!
Find the word and color it in.

may	me	may
mad	may	month

8 TELL IT!
Who did you tell?

_____

Go tell someone the word!

© Plush Education

17

SIGHT WORDS

Each word you learn is a treasure in your mind.

1 READ IT!

me

Say the word out loud.

2 COLOR IT!

me

Color in the word.

3 TRACE IT!

me

Trace the word.

4 WRITE IT!

Write the word.

5 SPELL IT!

Spell the word.

6 CLAP IT!

① ② ③

How many syllables are in the word? Color in the correct number.

7 FIND IT!

Find the word and color it in.

| me | mo | me |
| mi | me | my |

8 TELL IT!

Who did you tell?

Go tell someone the word!

SIGHT WORDS

"Keep learning — your brain loves it!"

1. READ IT!
my

Say the word out loud.

2. COLOR IT!
my

Color in the word.

3. TRACE IT!
my

Trace the word.

4. WRITE IT!

Write the word.

5. SPELL IT!

Spell the word.

6. CLAP IT!
1 2 3

How many syllables are in the word?
Color in the correct number.

7. FIND IT!
Find the word and color it in.

| my | me | my |
| mi | mo | my |

8. TELL IT!
Who did you tell?

_____

Go tell someone the word!

SIGHT WORDS

"Every great reader started just like you!"

1 READ IT!
no

Say the word out loud.

2 COLOR IT!
no

Color in the word.

3 TRACE IT!
no

Trace the word.

4 WRITE IT!

Write the word.

5 SPELL IT!

Spell the word.

6 CLAP IT!
1 2 3

How many syllables are in the word? Color in the correct number.

7 FIND IT!
Find the word and color it in.

off	no	off
no	on	no

8 TELL IT!
Who did you tell?

Go tell someone the word!

© Plush Education

SIGHT WORDS

You are a sight word star — keep shining!

1 READ IT!
of

Say the word out loud.

2 COLOR IT!
of

Color in the word.

3 TRACE IT!
of

Trace the word.

4 WRITE IT!

Write the word.

5 SPELL IT!

Spell the word.

6 CLAP IT!
1 2 3

How many syllables are in the word?
Color in the correct number.

7 FIND IT!

Find the word and color it in.

on	of	ok
of	off	of

8 TELL IT!

Who did you tell?

_____

Go tell someone the word!

21

© Plush Education

SIGHT WORDS

Don't be afraid to try — every word is practice.

1 READ IT!

on

Say the word out loud.

2 COLOR IT!

on

Color In the word.

3 TRACE IT!

on

Trace the word.

4 WRITE IT!

Write the word.

5 SPELL IT!

Spell the word.

6 CLAP IT!

1 2 3

How many syllables are In the word? Color In the correct number.

7 FIND IT!

Find the word and color it in.

| to | on | mo |
| on | on | no |

8 TELL IT!

Who did you tell?

Go tell someone the word!

© Plush Education

SIGHT WORDS

"Writing takes time — and you're doing amazing!"

1 READ IT!
or

Say the word out loud.

2 COLOR IT!
or

Color In the word.

3 TRACE IT!
or

Trace the word.

4 WRITE IT!

Write the word.

5 SPELL IT!

Spell the word.

6 CLAP IT!
1 2 3

How many syllables are In the word? Color In the correct number.

7 FIND IT!
Find the word and color it in.

so	or	off
or	on	or

8 TELL IT!
Who did you tell?

Go tell someone the word!

SIGHT WORDS

Sight words are everywhere — now you can find them!

1. READ IT!

SO

Say the word out loud.

2. COLOR IT!

SO

Color in the word.

3. TRACE IT!

so

Trace the word.

4. WRITE IT!

Write the word.

5. SPELL IT!

☐ ☐

Spell the word.

6. CLAP IT!

① ② ③

How many syllables are in the word?
Color in the correct number.

7. FIND IT!

Find the word and color it in.

so	os	so
si	so	as

8. TELL IT!

Who did you tell?

_____

Go tell someone the word!

© Plush Education

24

SIGHT WORDS

"One word at a time, you're building reading power!"

1 READ IT!

to

Say the word out loud.

2 COLOR IT!

to

Color In the word.

3 TRACE IT!

to

Trace the word.

4 WRITE IT!

Write the word.

5 SPELL IT!

☐ ☐

Spell the word.

6 CLAP IT!

① ② ③

How many syllables are In the word? Color In the correct number.

7 FIND IT!

Find the word and color it in.

to	ta	to
to	th	tj

8 TELL IT!

Who did you tell?

_____

Go tell someone the word!

SIGHT WORDS

"Your effort is magic — keep using it!"

1 READ IT!

up

Say the word out loud.

2 COLOR IT!

up

Color in the word.

3 TRACE IT!

up

Trace the word.

4 WRITE IT!

Write the word.

5 SPELL IT!

Spell the word.

6 CLAP IT!

1　2　3

How many syllables are in the word?
Color in the correct number.

7 FIND IT!

Find the word and color it in.

| up | um | un |
| up | up | du |

8 TELL IT!

Who did you tell?

Go tell someone the word!

SIGHT WORDS

Be proud of every word you write.

1. READ IT!

we

Say the word out loud.

2. COLOR IT!

we

Color in the word.

3. TRACE IT!

we

Trace the word.

4. WRITE IT!

Write the word.

5. SPELL IT!

Spell the word.

6. CLAP IT!

1 2 3

How many syllables are in the word? Color in the correct number.

7. FIND IT!

Find the word and color it in.

| we | went | on |
| we | gift | go |

8. TELL IT!

Who did you tell?

Go tell someone the word!

27

SIGHT WORDS

"You're learning something wonderful — keep going!"

1. READ IT!
all

Say the word out loud.

2. COLOR IT!
all

Color in the word.

3. TRACE IT!
all

Trace the word.

4. WRITE IT!

Write the word.

5. SPELL IT!

Spell the word.

6. CLAP IT!
1   2   3

How many syllables are in the word?
Color in the correct number.

7. FIND IT!

Find the word and color it in.

| all | as | all |
| all | at | an |

8. TELL IT!

Who did you tell?

_____

Go tell someone the word!

SIGHT WORDS

Writing and reading are adventures — enjoy the journey!

1 READ IT!

and

Say the word out loud.

2 COLOR IT!

and

Color in the word.

3 TRACE IT!

and

Trace the word.

4 WRITE IT!

_____

- - - - - - - - - - - - - -

_____

Write the word.

5 SPELL IT!

☐ ☐ ☐

Spell the word.

6 CLAP IT!

① ② ③

How many syllables are in the word?
Color in the correct number.

7 FIND IT!

Find the word and color it in.

and	ant	and
arm	and	all

8 TELL IT!

Who did you tell?

_____

Go tell someone the word!

© Plush Education

SIGHT WORDS

Keep your eyes on the words — you're a reading hero!

1 READ IT!

are

Say the word out loud.

2 COLOR IT!

are

Color In the word.

3 TRACE IT!

are

Trace the word.

4 WRITE IT!

Write the word.

5 SPELL IT!

Spell the word.

6 CLAP IT!

1 2 3

How many syllables are In the word?
Color In the correct number.

7 FIND IT!

Find the word and color it in.

| an | are | at |
| are | all | an |

8 TELL IT!

Who did you tell?

Go tell someone the word!

30

© Plush Education

SIGHT WORDS

"You're not just learning words — you're learning for life!"

1 READ IT!

big

Say the word out loud.

2 COLOR IT!

big

Color in the word.

3 TRACE IT!

big

Trace the word.

4 WRITE IT!

Write the word.

5 SPELL IT!

Spell the word.

6 CLAP IT!

1   2   3

How many syllables are in the word?
Color in the correct number.

7 FIND IT!

Find the word and color it in.

big	bad	big
big	bam	bag

8 TELL IT!

Who did you tell?

_____

Go tell someone the word!

© Plush Education

31

SIGHT WORDS

Reading sight words helps your brain grow strong!

1 READ IT!

but

Say the word out loud.

2 COLOR IT!

but

Color in the word.

3 TRACE IT!

but

Trace the word.

4 WRITE IT!

Write the word.

5 SPELL IT!

☐ ☐ ☐

Spell the word.

6 CLAP IT!

1   2   3

How many syllables are in the word?
Color in the correct number.

7 FIND IT!

Find the word and color it in.

| but | bad | bat |
| bag | but | but |

8 TELL IT!

Who did you tell?

_____

Go tell someone the word!

© Plush Education

32

SIGHT WORDS

Keep up the great work — you're doing awesome!

1. READ IT!

day

Say the word out loud.

2. COLOR IT!

day

Color in the word.

3. TRACE IT!

day

Trace the word.

4. WRITE IT!

Write the word.

5. SPELL IT!

Spell the word.

6. CLAP IT!

1   2   3

How many syllables are in the word?
Color in the correct number.

7. FIND IT!

Find the word and color it in.

date	day	did
day	do	day

8. TELL IT!

Who did you tell?

_____

Go tell someone the word!

33

SIGHT WORDS

"Your pencil is your tool — create with it!"

1 READ IT!

did

Say the word out loud.

2 COLOR IT!

did

Color in the word.

3 TRACE IT!

did

Trace the word.

4 WRITE IT!

Write the word.

5 SPELL IT!

Spell the word.

6 CLAP IT!

1 2 3

How many syllables are in the word? Color in the correct number.

7 FIND IT!

Find the word and color it in.

| dad | did | Warm |
| did | dam | dad |

8 TELL IT!

Who did you tell?

_____

Go tell someone the word!

SIGHT WORDS

You're a writer in the making — keep writing!

1 READ IT!
for

Say the word out loud.

2 COLOR IT!
for

Color in the word.

3 TRACE IT!
for

Trace the word.

4 WRITE IT!

Write the word.

5 SPELL IT!

☐ ☐ ☐

Spell the word.

6 CLAP IT!

① ② ③

How many syllables are in the word? Color in the correct number.

7 FIND IT!
Find the word and color it in.

for	for	fab
for	fam	for

8 TELL IT!
Who did you tell?

_____

Go tell someone the word!

© Plush Education

35

SIGHT WORDS

Smart kids like you practise sight words every day!

1 READ IT!
get

Say the word out loud.

2 COLOR IT!
get

Color In the word.

3 TRACE IT!
get

Trace the word.

4 WRITE IT!

Write the word.

5 SPELL IT!

Spell the word.

6 CLAP IT!
1 2 3

How many syllables are In the word? Color In the correct number.

7 FIND IT!
Find the word and color it in.

gad	get	gap
get	gam	get

8 TELL IT!
Who did you tell?

_____

Go tell someone the word!

36

© Plush Education

SIGHT WORDS

Every time you read a word, you win!

1 READ IT!

had

Say the word out loud.

2 COLOR IT!

had

Color In the word.

3 TRACE IT!

had

Trace the word.

4 WRITE IT!

Write the word.

5 SPELL IT!

Spell the word.

6 CLAP IT!

1   2   3

How many syllables are In the word?
Color In the correct number.

7 FIND IT!

Find the word and color it in.

| hen | had | hem |
| had | had | har |

8 TELL IT!

Who did you tell?

Go tell someone the word!

© Plush Education

37

SIGHT WORDS

Write today, shine tomorrow!

1 READ IT!

has

Say the word out loud.

2 COLOR IT!

has

Color In the word.

3 TRACE IT!

has

Trace the word.

4 WRITE IT!

Write the word.

5 SPELL IT!

Spell the word.

6 CLAP IT!

① ② ③

How many syllables are In the word? Color In the correct number.

7 FIND IT!

Find the word and color it in.

| have | hat | has |
| hat | has | have |

8 TELL IT!

Who did you tell?

_____

Go tell someone the word!

SIGHT WORDS

Words are your friends — get to know them!

1 READ IT!

her

Say the word out loud.

2 COLOR IT!

her

Color in the word.

3 TRACE IT!

her

Trace the word.

4 WRITE IT!

Write the word.

5 SPELL IT!

Spell the word.

6 CLAP IT!

1   2   3

How many syllables are in the word?
Color in the correct number.

7 FIND IT!

Find the word and color it in.

| has | her | hap |
| her | her | han |

8 TELL IT!

Who did you tell?

_____

Go tell someone the word!

© Plush Education

39

SIGHT WORDS

You've got the power — reading and writing power!

1 READ IT!
him
Say the word out loud.

2 COLOR IT!
him
Color in the word.

3 TRACE IT!
him
Trace the word.

4 WRITE IT!
Write the word.

5 SPELL IT!
Spell the word.

6 CLAP IT!
① ② ③
How many syllables are in the word? Color in the correct number.

7 FIND IT!
Find the word and color it in.

| him | had | hat |
| his | him | him |

8 TELL IT!
Who did you tell?

_____
Go tell someone the word!

40

© Plush Education

SIGHT WORDS

Keep going — sight words are getting easier!

1 READ IT!

his

Say the word out loud.

2 COLOR IT!

his

Color In the word.

3 TRACE IT!

his

Trace the word.

4 WRITE IT!

Write the word.

5 SPELL IT!

Spell the word.

6 CLAP IT!

1   2   3

How many syllables are In the word?
Color In the correct number.

7 FIND IT!

Find the word and color it in.

him	his	her
his	hut	his

8 TELL IT!

Who did you tell?

_____

Go tell someone the word!

41

SIGHT WORDS

"You're doing better than you think — keep it up!"

1 READ IT!

how

Say the word out loud.

2 COLOR IT!

how

Color in the word.

3 TRACE IT!

how

Trace the word.

4 WRITE IT!

Write the word.

5 SPELL IT!

Spell the word.

6 CLAP IT!

1   2   3

How many syllables are in the word?
Color in the correct number.

7 FIND IT!

Find the word and color it in.

| how | he | how |
| had | how | has |

8 TELL IT!

Who did you tell?

Go tell someone the word!

SIGHT WORDS

"Writing your best is what matters most."

1. READ IT!
its
Say the word out loud.

2. COLOR IT!
its
Color in the word.

3. TRACE IT!
its
Trace the word.

4. WRITE IT!
Write the word.

5. SPELL IT!
☐ ☐ ☐
Spell the word.

6. CLAP IT!
1 2 3
How many syllables are in the word? Color in the correct number.

7. FIND IT!
Find the word and color it in.

it	its	is
its	in	its

8. TELL IT!
Who did you tell?
_____
Go tell someone the word!

SIGHT WORDS

Read, write, repeat — that's how you grow!

1 READ IT!

not

Say the word out loud.

2 COLOR IT!

not

Color In the word.

3 TRACE IT!

not
‾‾‾‾‾‾‾‾‾‾‾‾

Trace the word.

4 WRITE IT!

Write the word.

5 SPELL IT!

☐ ☐ ☐

Spell the word.

6 CLAP IT!

① ② ③

How many syllables are In the word?
Color In the correct number.

7 FIND IT!

Find the word and color it in.

| not | nab | not |
| not | nay | nae |

8 TELL IT!

Who did you tell?

‾‾‾‾‾‾‾‾‾‾‾‾‾‾‾‾

Go tell someone the word!

SIGHT WORDS

"You're brave, smart, and ready to learn!"

1. READ IT!
now

Say the word out loud.

2. COLOR IT!
now

Color in the word.

3. TRACE IT!
now

Trace the word.

4. WRITE IT!

Write the word.

5. SPELL IT!

Spell the word.

6. CLAP IT!
1   2   3

How many syllables are in the word? Color in the correct number.

7. FIND IT!

Find the word and color it in.

now	new	now
not	now	no

8. TELL IT!

Who did you tell?

Go tell someone the word!

45

SIGHT WORDS

"Your hard work is showing — great job!"

1. READ IT!

one

Say the word out loud.

2. COLOR IT!

one

Color in the word.

3. TRACE IT!

one

Trace the word.

4. WRITE IT!

Write the word.

5. SPELL IT!

☐ ☐ ☐

Spell the word.

6. CLAP IT!

① ② ③

How many syllables are in the word?
Color in the correct number.

7. FIND IT!

Find the word and color it in.

| one | on | one |
| on | one | to |

8. TELL IT!

Who did you tell?

_____

Go tell someone the word!

46

SIGHT WORDS

With each word, you're becoming a stronger reader.

1 READ IT!

out

Say the word out loud.

2 COLOR IT!

out

Color in the word.

3 TRACE IT!

out

Trace the word.

4 WRITE IT!

Write the word.

5 SPELL IT!

Spell the word.

6 CLAP IT!

① ② ③

How many syllables are in the word? Color in the correct number.

7 FIND IT!

Find the word and color it in.

| out | oil | own |
| ons | out | out |

8 TELL IT!

Who did you tell?

Go tell someone the word!

© Plush Education

SIGHT WORDS

"Be patient — learning takes time and you're doing great!"

1 READ IT!

see

Say the word out loud.

2 COLOR IT!

see

Color in the word.

3 TRACE IT!

see

Trace the word.

4 WRITE IT!

Write the word.

5 SPELL IT!

Spell the word.

6 CLAP IT!

① ② ③

How many syllables are in the word?
Color in the correct number.

7 FIND IT!

Find the word and color it in.

| sod | see | sos |
| see | sew | see |

8 TELL IT!

Who did you tell?

Go tell someone the word!

© Plush Education

48

SIGHT WORDS

Celebrate your progress — every word counts!

1 READ IT!

she

Say the word out loud.

2 COLOR IT!

she

Color in the word.

3 TRACE IT!

she

Trace the word.

4 WRITE IT!

Write the word.

5 SPELL IT!

Spell the word.

6 CLAP IT!

1 2 3

How many syllables are in the word? Color in the correct number.

7 FIND IT!

Find the word and color it in.

she	her	she
see	his	he

8 TELL IT!

Who did you tell?

Go tell someone the word!

© Plush Education

49

SIGHT WORDS

Let your words fly — write with joy!

1 READ IT!

the

Say the word out loud.

2 COLOR IT!

the

Color In the word.

3 TRACE IT!

the

Trace the word.

4 WRITE IT!

Write the word.

5 SPELL IT!

Spell the word.

6 CLAP IT!

1   2   3

How many syllables are In the word? Color In the correct number.

7 FIND IT!

Find the word and color it in.

| the | the | tag |
| to | ted | the |

8 TELL IT!

Who did you tell?

_____

Go tell someone the word!

© Plush Education

SIGHT WORDS

"You're amazing — keep reaching for the stars!"

1 READ IT!

two

Say the word out loud.

2 COLOR IT!

two

Color in the word.

3 TRACE IT!

two

Trace the word.

4 WRITE IT!

_____

Write the word.

5 SPELL IT!

☐ ☐ ☐

Spell the word.

6 CLAP IT!

① ② ③

How many syllables are in the word? Color in the correct number.

7 FIND IT!

Find the word and color it in.

the	two	there
two	tree	two

8 TELL IT!

Who did you tell?

_____

Go tell someone the word!

© Plush Education

SIGHT WORDS

"Little by little, you're mastering those words!"

1 READ IT!

use

Say the word out loud.

2 COLOR IT!

use

Color in the word.

3 TRACE IT!

use

Trace the word.

4 WRITE IT!

Write the word.

5 SPELL IT!

Spell the word.

6 CLAP IT!

① ② ③

How many syllables are in the word?
Color in the correct number.

7 FIND IT!

Find the word and color it in.

use	up	use
es	use	up

8 TELL IT!

Who did you tell?

_____

Go tell someone the word!

© Plush Education

SIGHT WORDS

Keep shining — sight word master in the making!

1 READ IT!

was

Say the word out loud.

2 COLOR IT!

was

Color in the word.

3 TRACE IT!

was

Trace the word.

4 WRITE IT!

Write the word.

5 SPELL IT!

Spell the word.

6 CLAP IT!

1　2　3

How many syllables are in the word? Color in the correct number.

7 FIND IT!

Find the word and color it in.

| was | that | was |
| war | was | wan |

8 TELL IT!

Who did you tell?

_____

Go tell someone the word!

53

© Plush Education

SIGHT WORDS

"You are unstoppable — words can't wait to meet you!"

1 READ IT!

who

Say the word out loud.

2 COLOR IT!

who

Color in the word.

3 TRACE IT!

who

Trace the word.

4 WRITE IT!

Write the word.

5 SPELL IT!

Spell the word.

6 CLAP IT!

1   2   3

How many syllables are in the word? Color in the correct number.

7 FIND IT!

Find the word and color it in.

| who | where | who |
| when | who | what |

8 TELL IT!

Who did you tell?

Go tell someone the word!

SIGHT WORDS

"Keep practising — you're one step closer to becoming a sight word pro!"

1 READ IT!

will

Say the word out loud.

2 COLOR IT!

will

Color in the word.

3 TRACE IT!

Trace the word.

4 WRITE IT!

_____

- -

_____

Write the word.

5 SPELL IT!

☐ ☐ ☐ ☐

Spell the word.

6 CLAP IT!

① ② ③

How many syllables are in the word?
Color in the correct number.

7 FIND IT!

Find the word and color it in.

was	will	war
will	wai	will

8 TELL IT!

Who did you tell?

_____

Go tell someone the word!

55

© Plush Education

SIGHT WORDS

Every word you learn is a victory!

1 READ IT!
yes
Say the word out loud.

2 COLOR IT!
yes
Color in the word.

3 TRACE IT!
yes
Trace the word.

4 WRITE IT!
_____
_____
Write the word.

5 SPELL IT!
☐ ☐ ☐ ☐
Spell the word.

6 CLAP IT!
① ② ③
How many syllables are in the word?
Color in the correct number.

7 FIND IT!
Find the word and color it in.

yes	yad	yet
yaa	yes	yes

8 TELL IT!
Who did you tell?

_____

Go tell someone the word!

SIGHT WORDS

"Writing is a journey — enjoy every step you take."

1. READ IT!
you
Say the word out loud.

2. COLOR IT!
you
Color in the word.

3. TRACE IT!
you
Trace the word.

4. WRITE IT!
Write the word.

5. SPELL IT!
☐ ☐ ☐
Spell the word.

6. CLAP IT!
1 2 3
How many syllables are in the word?
Color in the correct number.

7. FIND IT!
Find the word and color it in.

| yes | yet | you |
| he | you | yak |

8. TELL IT!
Who did you tell?

_____

Go tell someone the word!

© Plush Education

SIGHT WORDS

"Don't stop now — you're getting better with every word!"

1. READ IT!
been
Say the word out loud.

2. COLOR IT!
been
Color In the word.

3. TRACE IT!
been
Trace the word.

4. WRITE IT!
Write the word.

5. SPELL IT!
☐ ☐ ☐ ☐
Spell the word.

6. CLAP IT!
① ② ③
How many syllables are In the word? Color In the correct number.

7. FIND IT!
Find the word and color it in.

| been | bee | been |
| bee | been | bee |

8. TELL IT!
Who did you tell?

_____

Go tell someone the word!

58

© Plush Education

SIGHT WORDS

"Learning sight words is fun — keep discovering new ones!"

1. READ IT!
call
Say the word out loud.

2. COLOR IT!
call
Color in the word.

3. TRACE IT!
call
Trace the word.

4. WRITE IT!
Write the word.

5. SPELL IT!
☐ ☐ ☐ ☐
Spell the word.

6. CLAP IT!
1 2 3
How many syllables are in the word? Color in the correct number.

7. FIND IT!
Find the word and color it in.

all	call	car
call	cat	all

8. TELL IT!
Who did you tell?

_____

Go tell someone the word!

© Plush Education

SIGHT WORDS

"You're doing amazing — every word you write counts!"

1. READ IT!
come
Say the word out loud.

2. COLOR IT!
come
Color in the word.

3. TRACE IT!
come
Trace the word.

4. WRITE IT!
Write the word.

5. SPELL IT!
☐ ☐ ☐ ☐
Spell the word.

6. CLAP IT!
① ② ③
How many syllables are in the word?
Color in the correct number.

7. FIND IT!
Find the word and color it in.

| clay | come | come |
| come | cake | crow |

8. TELL IT!
Who did you tell?

_____

Go tell someone the word!

© Plush Education

60

SIGHT WORDS

"The more you read, the more words you'll know!"

1 READ IT!

could

Say the word out loud.

2 COLOR IT!

could

Color In the word.

3 TRACE IT!

could

Trace the word.

4 WRITE IT!

Write the word.

5 SPELL IT!

☐ ☐ ☐ ☐ ☐

Spell the word.

6 CLAP IT!

1 2 3

How many syllables are In the word? Color In the correct number.

7 FIND IT!

Find the word and color it in.

could	then	could
cabin	could	caber

8 TELL IT!

Who did you tell?

_____

Go tell someone the word!

61

SIGHT WORDS

Great writers don't give up — neither do you!

1 READ IT!

down

Say the word out loud.

2 COLOR IT!

down

Color in the word.

3 TRACE IT!

down

Trace the word.

4 WRITE IT!

Write the word.

5 SPELL IT!

☐ ☐ ☐ ☐

Spell the word.

6 CLAP IT!

① ② ③

How many syllables are in the word? Color in the correct number.

7 FIND IT!

Find the word and color it in.

| down | down | duck |
| doll | down | dog |

8 TELL IT!

Who did you tell?

_____

Go tell someone the word!

© Plush Education

62

SIGHT WORDS

"Keep your eyes on the words — you're becoming a reading superstar!"

1 READ IT!

each

Say the word out loud.

2 COLOR IT!

each

Color In the word.

3 TRACE IT!

each

Trace the word.

4 WRITE IT!

Write the word.

5 SPELL IT!

Spell the word.

6 CLAP IT!

1 2 3

How many syllables are In the word?
Color In the correct number.

7 FIND IT!

Find the word and color it in.

| an | each | eat |
| each | all | each |

8 TELL IT!

Who did you tell?

Go tell someone the word!

63

© Plush Education

SIGHT WORDS

Every new word you learn makes you a better reader!

1 READ IT!
first
Say the word out loud.

2 COLOR IT!
first
Color in the word.

3 TRACE IT!
first
Trace the word.

4 WRITE IT!
Write the word.

5 SPELL IT!
Spell the word.

6 CLAP IT!
1   2   3
How many syllables are in the word? Color in the correct number.

7 FIND IT!
Find the word and color it in.

| first | fish | first |
| feet | fear | fast |

8 TELL IT!
Who did you tell?

Go tell someone the word!

64

© Plush Education

SIGHT WORDS

Don't rush — take your time and enjoy the learning process.

1. READ IT!

from

Say the word out loud.

2. COLOR IT!

from

Color in the word.

3. TRACE IT!

from

Trace the word.

4. WRITE IT!

Write the word.

5. SPELL IT!

☐ ☐ ☐ ☐

Spell the word.

6. CLAP IT!

① ② ③

How many syllables are in the word? Color in the correct number.

7. FIND IT!

Find the word and color it in.

| from | form | from |
| off | from | on |

8. TELL IT!

Who did you tell?

_____

Go tell someone the word!

65

SIGHT WORDS

"You're building a strong foundation for your reading and writing skills!"

1 READ IT!
have
Say the word out loud.

2 COLOR IT!
have
Color In the word.

3 TRACE IT!
have
Trace the word.

4 WRITE IT!
Write the word.

5 SPELL IT!
☐ ☐ ☐ ☐
Spell the word.

6 CLAP IT!
① ② ③
How many syllables are In the word?
Color In the correct number.

7 FIND IT!
Find the word and color it in.

have	had	have
has	have	hand

8 TELL IT!
Who did you tell?
_____
Go tell someone the word!

66

© Plush Education

SIGHT WORDS

Learning sight words is like collecting treasures for your brain!

1 READ IT!

into

Say the word out loud.

2 COLOR IT!

into

Color In the word.

3 TRACE IT!

into

Trace the word.

4 WRITE IT!

Write the word.

5 SPELL IT!

Spell the word.

6 CLAP IT!

1　2　3

How many syllables are In the word? Color In the correct number.

7 FIND IT!

Find the word and color it in.

irky	into	icon
into	info	into

8 TELL IT!

Who did you tell?

_____

Go tell someone the word!

67

© Plush Education

SIGHT WORDS

"You're unlocking the world of words — keep going!"

1 READ IT!
just

Say the word out loud.

2 COLOR IT!
just

Color in the word.

3 TRACE IT!
just

Trace the word.

4 WRITE IT!

Write the word.

5 SPELL IT!

Spell the word.

6 CLAP IT!
1   2   3

How many syllables are in the word? Color in the correct number.

7 FIND IT!
Find the word and color it in.

| July | just | jabs |
| just | Jack | just |

8 TELL IT!
Who did you tell?

_____

Go tell someone the word!

68

SIGHT WORDS

Every word you write is like a puzzle piece — you're completing the picture!

1 READ IT!

like

Say the word out loud.

2 COLOR IT!

like

Color in the word.

3 TRACE IT!

like

Trace the word.

4 WRITE IT!

Write the word.

5 SPELL IT!

☐ ☐ ☐ ☐

Spell the word.

6 CLAP IT!

① ② ③

How many syllables are in the word? Color in the correct number.

7 FIND IT!

Find the word and color it in.

like	Lock	Lark
Lily	like	like

8 TELL IT!

Who did you tell?

_____

Go tell someone the word!

69

© Plush Education

SIGHT WORDS

"Keep going — each word brings you closer to your goal!"

1 READ IT!

little

Say the word out loud.

2 COLOR IT!

little

Color in the word.

3 TRACE IT!

little

Trace the word.

4 WRITE IT!

Write the word.

5 SPELL IT!

Spell the word.

6 CLAP IT!

1   2   3

How many syllables are in the word?
Color in the correct number.

7 FIND IT!

Find the word and color it in.

| little | then | luck |
| little | ten | little |

8 TELL IT!

Who did you tell?

Go tell someone the word!

SIGHT WORDS

Every letter you write brings you closer to being a master writer!

1 READ IT!

long

Say the word out loud.

2 COLOR IT!

long

Color in the word.

3 TRACE IT!

Trace the word.

4 WRITE IT!

Write the word.

5 SPELL IT!

Spell the word.

6 CLAP IT!

① ② ③

How many syllables are in the word?
Color in the correct number.

7 FIND IT!

Find the word and color it in.

| long | List | long |
| Love | long | Lone |

8 TELL IT!

Who did you tell?

_____

Go tell someone the word!

© Plush Education

SIGHT WORDS

Believe in your words — they will help you grow.

1 READ IT!

look

Say the word out loud.

2 COLOR IT!

look

Color in the word.

3 TRACE IT!

look

Trace the word.

4 WRITE IT!

Write the word.

5 SPELL IT!

Spell the word.

6 CLAP IT!

1   2   3

How many syllables are in the word?
Color in the correct number.

7 FIND IT!

Find the word and color it in.

| Lamp | look | look |
| look | Lily | Link |

8 TELL IT!

Who did you tell?

_____

Go tell someone the word!

© Plush Education

SIGHT WORDS

Every time you read, you learn something new — keep reading!

1. READ IT!

made

Say the word out loud.

2. COLOR IT!

made

Color In the word.

3. TRACE IT!

made

Trace the word.

4. WRITE IT!

Write the word.

5. SPELL IT!

☐ ☐ ☐ ☐

Spell the word.

6. CLAP IT!

① ② ③

How many syllables are In the word? Color In the correct number.

7. FIND IT!

Find the word and color it in.

| made | mad | made |
| mall | made | man |

8. TELL IT!

Who did you tell?

_____

Go tell someone the word!

SIGHT WORDS

"You are getting smarter every time you write and read!"

1. READ IT!
many
Say the word out loud.

2. COLOR IT!
many
Color in the word.

3. TRACE IT!
many
Trace the word.

4. WRITE IT!
Write the word.

5. SPELL IT!
Spell the word.

6. CLAP IT!
1 2 3
How many syllables are in the word? Color in the correct number.

7. FIND IT!
Find the word and color it in.

| many | man | many |
| mad | many | made |

8. TELL IT!
Who did you tell?

Go tell someone the word!

© Plush Education

74

SIGHT WORDS

Write with pride — every word is a step forward!

1. READ IT!
more
Say the word out loud.

2. COLOR IT!
more
Color in the word.

3. TRACE IT!
more
Trace the word.

4. WRITE IT!

Write the word.

5. SPELL IT!
☐ ☐ ☐ ☐
Spell the word.

6. CLAP IT!
① ② ③
How many syllables are in the word? Color in the correct number.

7. FIND IT!
Find the word and color it in.

| an | am | off |
| am | all | am |

8. TELL IT!
Who did you tell?

_____

Go tell someone the word!

75

© Plush Education

SIGHT WORDS

Keep practising your sight words and see how far you can go!

1 READ IT!

over

Say the word out loud.

2 COLOR IT!

over

Color In the word.

3 TRACE IT!

over

Trace the word.

4 WRITE IT!

Write the word.

5 SPELL IT!

Spell the word.

6 CLAP IT!

1 2 3

How many syllables are In the word? Color In the correct number.

7 FIND IT!

Find the word and color it in.

| over | obey | over |
| omit | over | opal |

8 TELL IT!

Who did you tell?

Go tell someone the word!

SIGHT WORDS

Your imagination and your words are limitless!

1 READ IT!

ride

Say the word out loud.

2 COLOR IT!

ride

Color in the word.

3 TRACE IT!

ride

Trace the word.

4 WRITE IT!

_____

Write the word.

5 SPELL IT!

☐ ☐ ☐ ☐

Spell the word.

6 CLAP IT!

① ② ③

How many syllables are in the word? Color in the correct number.

7 FIND IT!

Find the word and color it in.

ride	Race	ride
ride	Rage	Racy

8 TELL IT!

Who did you tell?

_____

Go tell someone the word!

SIGHT WORDS

"Every word you master is another victory on your path to greatness!"

1 READ IT!
said
Say the word out loud.

2 COLOR IT!
said
Color in the word.

3 TRACE IT!
said
Trace the word.

4 WRITE IT!
Write the word.

5 SPELL IT!
Spell the word.

6 CLAP IT!
1 2 3
How many syllables are in the word? Color in the correct number.

7 FIND IT!
Find the word and color it in.

| said | said | Shoe |
| said | Side | Salt |

8 TELL IT!
Who did you tell?

Go tell someone the word!

78

© Plush Education

SIGHT WORDS

Write your dreams — sight words will help you tell your story!

1 READ IT!

some

Say the word out loud.

2 COLOR IT!

some

Color in the word.

3 TRACE IT!

some

Trace the word.

4 WRITE IT!

Write the word.

5 SPELL IT!

☐ ☐ ☐ ☐

Spell the word.

6 CLAP IT!

1   2   3

How many syllables are in the word? Color in the correct number.

7 FIND IT!

Find the word and color it in.

| Shot | some | some |
| some | Swim | Ship |

8 TELL IT!

Who did you tell?

_____

Go tell someone the word!

SIGHT WORDS

"Reading and writing is a team effort — you and your words are a great team!"

1 READ IT!

than

Say the word out loud.

2 COLOR IT!

than

Color in the word.

3 TRACE IT!

than

Trace the word.

4 WRITE IT!

Write the word.

5 SPELL IT!

☐ ☐ ☐ ☐

Spell the word.

6 CLAP IT!

① ② ③

How many syllables are in the word?
Color in the correct number.

7 FIND IT!

Find the word and color it in.

that	than	that
than	the	than

8 TELL IT!

Who did you tell?

_____

Go tell someone the word!

80

SIGHT WORDS

"Keep shining, one word at a time!"

1 READ IT!

that

Say the word out loud.

2 COLOR IT!

that

Color In the word.

3 TRACE IT!

that

Trace the word.

4 WRITE IT!

Write the word.

5 SPELL IT!

Spell the word.

6 CLAP IT!

1   2   3

How many syllables are In the word?
Color In the correct number.

7 FIND IT!

Find the word and color it in.

| Twit | that | that |
| that | Tree | Toss |

8 TELL IT!

Who did you tell?

_____

Go tell someone the word!

© Plush Education

81

SIGHT WORDS

"Don't worry about mistakes — they help you get better!"

1 READ IT!

their

Say the word out loud.

2 COLOR IT!

their

Color in the word.

3 TRACE IT!

their

Trace the word.

4 WRITE IT!

Write the word.

5 SPELL IT!

☐ ☐ ☐ ☐ ☐

Spell the word.

6 CLAP IT!

① ② ③

How many syllables are in the word? Color in the correct number.

7 FIND IT!

Find the word and color it in.

| there | their | that |
| their | these | their |

8 TELL IT!

Who did you tell?

_____

Go tell someone the word!

© Plush Education

SIGHT WORDS

The more sight words you know, the more you can read and understand!

1 READ IT!

them

Say the word out loud.

2 COLOR IT!

them

Color in the word.

3 TRACE IT!

them

Trace the word.

4 WRITE IT!

Write the word.

5 SPELL IT!

☐ ☐ ☐ ☐

Spell the word.

6 CLAP IT!

① ② ③

How many syllables are in the word? Color in the correct number.

7 FIND IT!

Find the word and color it in.

| trip | them | turn |
| them | toss | them |

8 TELL IT!

Who did you tell?

_____

Go tell someone the word!

83

SIGHT WORDS

"You are amazing at learning sight words — keep up the great work!"

1 READ IT!

then

Say the word out loud.

2 COLOR IT!

then

Color in the word.

3 TRACE IT!

then

Trace the word.

4 WRITE IT!

Write the word.

5 SPELL IT!

☐ ☐ ☐ ☐

Spell the word.

6 CLAP IT!

① ② ③

How many syllables are in the word?
Color in the correct number.

7 FIND IT!

Find the word and color it in.

| then | the | thank |
| then | tell | then |

8 TELL IT!

Who did you tell?

_____

Go tell someone the word!

SIGHT WORDS

"Writing is like building — one word at a time, you're creating something big!"

1. READ IT!

there

Say the word out loud.

2. COLOR IT!

there

Color in the word.

3. TRACE IT!

there

Trace the word.

4. WRITE IT!

Write the word.

5. SPELL IT!

☐ ☐ ☐ ☐ ☐

Spell the word.

6. CLAP IT!

① ② ③

How many syllables are in the word?
Color in the correct number.

7. FIND IT!

Find the word and color it in.

| there | there | taboo |
| tabby | there | table |

8. TELL IT!

Who did you tell?

_____

Go tell someone the word!

SIGHT WORDS

Each word you write brings you closer to being a reading expert!

1 READ IT!
these
Say the word out loud.

2 COLOR IT!
these
Color In the word.

3 TRACE IT!
these
Trace the word.

4 WRITE IT!

Write the word.

5 SPELL IT!
☐ ☐ ☐ ☐ ☐
Spell the word.

6 CLAP IT!
① ② ③
How many syllables are In the word?
Color In the correct number.

7 FIND IT!
Find the word and color it in.

there	these	that
these	this	these

8 TELL IT!
Who did you tell?

_____

Go tell someone the word!

86

SIGHT WORDS

You are a word wizard — watch your words come to life!

1 READ IT!
they

Say the word out loud.

2 COLOR IT!
they

Color In the word.

3 TRACE IT!
they

Trace the word.

4 WRITE IT!

Write the word.

5 SPELL IT!

☐ ☐ ☐ ☐

Spell the word.

6 CLAP IT!
① ② ③

How many syllables are In the word?
Color In the correct number.

7 FIND IT!
Find the word and color it in.

| Thud | they | Temp |
| they | Trek | they |

8 TELL IT!
Who did you tell?

_____

Go tell someone the word!

87

© Plush Education

SIGHT WORDS

"The more sight words you learn, the easier reading will become!"

1 READ IT!

this

Say the word out loud.

2 COLOR IT!

this

Color in the word.

3 TRACE IT!

this

Trace the word.

4 WRITE IT!

Write the word.

5 SPELL IT!

Spell the word.

6 CLAP IT!

1 2 3

How many syllables are in the word?
Color in the correct number.

7 FIND IT!

Find the word and color it in.

| trap | this | this |
| this | tilt | tend |

8 TELL IT!

Who did you tell?

_____

Go tell someone the word!

88

SIGHT WORDS

"You're doing fantastic — every word you learn brings you closer to your goal!"

1 READ IT!
time

Say the word out loud.

2 COLOR IT!
time

Color in the word.

3 TRACE IT!
time

Trace the word.

4 WRITE IT!

Write the word.

5 SPELL IT!

☐ ☐ ☐ ☐

Spell the word.

6 CLAP IT!
① ② ③

How many syllables are in the word? Color in the correct number.

7 FIND IT!
Find the word and color it in.

this	time	tip
time	that	time

8 TELL IT!
Who did you tell?

_____

Go tell someone the word!

© Plush Education

SIGHT WORDS

"The more you practice, the easier sight words will be!"

1 READ IT!
very
Say the word out loud.

2 COLOR IT!
very
Color In the word.

3 TRACE IT!
very
Trace the word.

4 WRITE IT!
_____
Write the word.

5 SPELL IT!
☐ ☐ ☐ ☐
Spell the word.

6 CLAP IT!
① ② ③
How many syllables are In the word? Color In the correct number.

7 FIND IT!
Find the word and color it in.

| vain | very | vacs |
| very | vale | very |

8 TELL IT!
Who did you tell?
_____
Go tell someone the word!

90

© Plush Education

SIGHT WORDS

Every sight word you know helps you become a better reader!

1 READ IT!

went

Say the word out loud.

2 COLOR IT!

went

Color in the word.

3 TRACE IT!

went

Trace the word.

4 WRITE IT!

Write the word.

5 SPELL IT!

☐ ☐ ☐ ☐

Spell the word.

6 CLAP IT!

① ② ③

How many syllables are in the word? Color in the correct number.

7 FIND IT!

Find the word and color it in.

| went | wale | went |
| walk | went | wait |

8 TELL IT!

Who did you tell?

_____

Go tell someone the word!

© Plush Education

SIGHT WORDS

With every word, you're improving your reading and writing skills!

1. READ IT!

were

Say the word out loud.

2. COLOR IT!

were

Color in the word.

3. TRACE IT!

were

Trace the word.

4. WRITE IT!

Write the word.

5. SPELL IT!

☐ ☐ ☐ ☐

Spell the word.

6. CLAP IT!

① ② ③

How many syllables are in the word?
Color in the correct number.

7. FIND IT!

Find the word and color it in.

| were | were | war |
| wag | wap | were |

8. TELL IT!

Who did you tell?

_____

Go tell someone the word!

SIGHT WORDS

Keep writing and reading — you're doing awesome!

1 READ IT!

what

Say the word out loud.

2 COLOR IT!

what

Color In the word.

3 TRACE IT!

what

Trace the word.

4 WRITE IT!

Write the word.

5 SPELL IT!

Spell the word.

6 CLAP IT!

1   2   3

How many syllables are In the word?
Color In the correct number.

7 FIND IT!

Find the word and color it in.

| what | Wolf | what |
| what | Water | Who |

8 TELL IT!

Who did you tell?

Go tell someone the word!

© Plush Education

93

SIGHT WORDS

"Your words have power — keep writing and let them shine!"

1. READ IT!

when

Say the word out loud.

2. COLOR IT!

when

Color in the word.

3. TRACE IT!

when

Trace the word.

4. WRITE IT!

Write the word.

5. SPELL IT!

☐ ☐ ☐ ☐

Spell the word.

6. CLAP IT!

① ② ③

How many syllables are in the word? Color in the correct number.

7. FIND IT!

Find the word and color it in.

| when | when | Warm |
| Wolf | when | Who |

8. TELL IT!

Who did you tell?

_____

Go tell someone the word!

SIGHT WORDS

"Your hard work is paying off — you're learning sight words like a pro!"

1. READ IT!
which
Say the word out loud.

2. COLOR IT!
which
Color in the word.

3. TRACE IT!
which
Trace the word.

4. WRITE IT!
Write the word.

5. SPELL IT!
☐ ☐ ☐ ☐ ☐
Spell the word.

6. CLAP IT!
1   2   3
How many syllables are in the word? Color in the correct number.

7. FIND IT!
Find the word and color it in.

| with | white | which |
| which | write | with |

8. TELL IT!
Who did you tell?

_____

Go tell someone the word!

SIGHT WORDS

Don't stop now — every sight word is a new achievement!

1. READ IT!

with

Say the word out loud.

2. COLOR IT!

with

Color In the word.

3. TRACE IT!

with

Trace the word.

4. WRITE IT!

_____

Write the word.

5. SPELL IT!

☐ ☐ ☐ ☐

Spell the word.

6. CLAP IT!

① ② ③

How many syllables are In the word? Color In the correct number.

7. FIND IT!

Find the word and color it in.

wack	with	with
with	wadi	wady

8. TELL IT!

Who did you tell?

_____

Go tell someone the word!

SIGHT WORDS

Keep writing and reading — you're becoming a word expert!

1 READ IT!

word

Say the word out loud.

2 COLOR IT!

word

Color in the word.

3 TRACE IT!

word

Trace the word.

4 WRITE IT!

Write the word.

5 SPELL IT!

Spell the word.

6 CLAP IT!

1   2   3

How many syllables are in the word?
Color in the correct number.

7 FIND IT!

Find the word and color it in.

| word | wool | word |
| would | word | who |

8 TELL IT!

Who did you tell?

Go tell someone the word!

SIGHT WORDS

"The more you read, the more you know — keep going!"

1 READ IT!

would

Say the word out loud.

2 COLOR IT!

would

Color in the word.

3 TRACE IT!

would

Trace the word.

4 WRITE IT!

Write the word.

5 SPELL IT!

☐ ☐ ☐ ☐ ☐

Spell the word.

6 CLAP IT!

① ② ③

How many syllables are in the word? Color in the correct number.

7 FIND IT!

Find the word and color it in.

would	wacky	would
wages	would	waits

8 TELL IT!

Who did you tell?

_____

Go tell someone the word!

98

SIGHT WORDS

"Each new word is a building block in your journey to success!"

1 READ IT!
write

Say the word out loud.

2 COLOR IT!
write

Color In the word.

3 TRACE IT!
write

Trace the word.

4 WRITE IT!

Write the word.

5 SPELL IT!

Spell the word.

6 CLAP IT!
1   2   3

How many syllables are In the word? Color In the correct number.

7 FIND IT!
Find the word and color it in.

| white | write | where |
| write | with | wat |

8 TELL IT!
Who did you tell?

Go tell someone the word!

SIGHT WORDS

You're mastering sight words — keep up the great work!

1. READ IT!

your

Say the word out loud.

2. COLOR IT!

your

Color in the word.

3. TRACE IT!

your

Trace the word.

4. WRITE IT!

Write the word.

5. SPELL IT!

☐ ☐ ☐ ☐

Spell the word.

6. CLAP IT!

① ② ③

How many syllables are in the word? Color in the correct number.

7. FIND IT!

Find the word and color it in.

| your | yolk | yawp |
| yang | your | your |

8. TELL IT!

Who did you tell?

_____

Go tell someone the word!

© Plush Education

100

CERTIFICATE OF ACHIEVEMENT

GREAT JOB!

This Certificate is Proudly Presented to:

(Name)

For Completing

READING & WRITING ADVENTURES: SIGHT WORDS FOR KIDS

You've taken your first big steps in learning 100 Sight Words, and that's something to be proud of. Sight words help you read with ease and write with confidence. Let this achievement remind you how amazing learning can be - keep exploring, keep practicing, and let your reading adventures continue to grow every day!

(Date)   **(Signature)**